WHAT PEOPLE ARE SAYING ABOUT *NOT EVEN A HINT* BY JOSHUA HARRIS

"This is a timely book. Josh boldly deals with the strongest attacks on young men and women today. It's hard to be God's man or God's woman when we continually feel and experience the failures of our sinful nature. This book is a practical call to personal holiness. I am happy to endorse such an endeavor."

CHRIS TOMLIN
SIXSTEP RECORDS ARTIST/WORSHIPER

"Full of wise, practical insight, this book offers help and hope—not just for those who are dealing with sexual lust, but for anyone besieged by temptation or battling besetting sins of any kind."

NANCY LEIGH DEMOSS, AUTHOR AND HOST OF THE *REVIVE OUR HEARTS* RADIO PROGRAM

"We cannot waste time playing hide-and-seek with lust and its consequences. Joshua Harris has earned our trust by talking straight and teaching from the Word of God. His wisdom on the true nature of lust will not only inform but challenge every Christian."

R. ALBERT MOHLER JR., PRESIDENT, SOUTHERN BAPTIST THEOLOGICAL SEMINARY

"I am very encouraged that my longtime friend Josh Harris has written a book about lust, speaking about the place where compromise begins—the mind. May God use this book to keep many from allowing their minds to become 'the devil's playground.'"

REBECCA ST. JAMES, SINGER/SONGWRITER

"The main issue with lust is that it hinders us from seeing and savoring the glory of Christ. That hurts us and dishonors Him. So, for your joy and Christ's honor, I commend this book to you. It is realistic, practical, and hope-giving because of uncompromising grace. T pure in heart will see God. If you want that sight, le⊥ you fight."

JOHN PIPER, BETHLEHEM BAPTIST CHU

"I may not have kissed dating goodbye, but *Not Even a Hint* is one of the most powerful books I've read. Josh writes honestly and transparently, giving practical counsel on fighting lust. This is an absolute must-read for anyone who is serious about living righteously."

JERAMY CLARK, AUTHOR OF *I GAVE DATING A CHANCE*

"Joshua Harris has done it again. You hold in your hand undiluted biblical truth on a vital topic, served up with honesty and humility. I'm not aware of another book quite like it."

C. J. MAHANEY, AUTHOR OF
THE CROSS CENTERED LIFE

"Wow! This book is guts and grace intertwined. *Not Even a Hint* is a work of colossal importance for both guys and girls. Our generation is in desperate need of this message."

ERIC AND LESLIE LUDY, AUTHORS OF
WHEN GOD WRITES YOUR LOVE STORY

"A beautiful blend of grace and truth. My friend Joshua Harris raises high standards of holiness while carefully avoiding legalism. Honest, biblical, and practical—I highly recommend it."

RANDY ALCORN, BESTSELLING AUTHOR OF
THE TREASURE PRINCIPLE AND *THE PURITY PRINCIPLE*

"Forthright, honest, and compelling. Joshua Harris has written a book about sexual purity that can be read and applied by both men and women. He shows us in practical and specific ways how we can grow toward God's standard—absolute purity in mind and body."

JERRY BRIDGES, AUTHOR OF
THE PURSUIT OF HOLINESS

SHANNON & JOSHUA HARRIS

WITH BRIAN SMITH

A STUDY GUIDE FOR WOMEN

not *even* a hint

Multnomah® Publishers *Sisters, Oregon*

NOT EVEN A HINT: A STUDY GUIDE FOR WOMEN
published by Multnomah Publishers, Inc.

© 2004 by Joshua and Shannon Harris
International Standard Book Number: 1-59052-354-7

Cover design by Steve Gardner/His Image Pixelworks
Cover image by PIER/Getty Images

Unless otherwise indicated, Scripture quotations are from:
The Holy Bible, New International Version
© 1973, 1984 by International Bible Society,
used by permission of Zondervan Publishing House
Other Scripture quotations are from:
The Holy Bible, English Standard Version (ESV)
© 2001 by Crossway Bibles, a division of Good News Publishers.
Used by permission. All rights reserved.

Multnomah is a trademark of Multnomah Publishers, Inc.,
and is registered in the U.S. Patent and Trademark Office.
The colophon is a trademark of Multnomah Publishers, Inc.

Printed in the United States of America

For information:
MULTNOMAH PUBLISHERS, INC.
POST OFFICE BOX 1720
SISTERS, OREGON 97759

04 05 06 07 08 09 10—10 9 8 7 6 5 4 3 2 1 0

Contents

Both Josh and I believe it's important to state from the outset that it was the hard work of Brian Smith that made this study guide possible. After Josh wrote *Not Even a Hint,* Brian took the time to both create the format of this study guide and write the questions. As you'll see, he has done a terrific job. My role was to add a feminine touch by writing an introduction for each chapter. But Brian did the majority of the work, and for that I'm very grateful.

Introduction

I f you're a woman who has decided to use this study guide for *Not Even a Hint,* I want to wholeheartedly applaud you. Contrary to what most of the world believes, lust is not just a guy problem; it is a human problem—a sin problem—and no one, male or female, single or married, is exempt from its snares. It takes humility to admit that you struggle with lust. But let me assure you that you are not the only woman to face this struggle. Even though I'm happily married, I am not above the temptations of lust. I must still guard my heart and mind as diligently as ever.

This study guide is designed for women who are serious about helping each other grow in holiness. It's designed to help us open an often hidden part of our lives for honest and godly discussion about female sexuality. Our sexuality is a beautiful and sacred gift from God. We want to be both thankful for it and respectful of God's commands to be pure. This study will challenge you to apply the principles of *Not Even a Hint* in your daily lives in order to guide you into the safety and joy of purity.

WHO CAN USE IT?

The *Not Even a Hint Study Guide for Women* is extremely versatile. It can be used in a group setting or individually. However, it is designed primarily for two or more women who want to work through the book together. Whether this is a group of three girlfriends that meets weekly at a coffee shop or a dozen women in a Sunday school class, this guide can be adapted to meet your needs.

There are different ways for a group to use it. One option is for each member to have her own copy of the study guide and to work through the appropriate lesson on her own before each meeting, writing her answers and then coming to the meeting ready to share. (This is ideal, since it encourages each woman to think through answers more carefully.)

The second option is for only the leader to have a copy of the study guide. With this approach, group members read the appropriate chapter in *Not Even a Hint* before the meeting, and then the leader uses the study guide to lead discussion. If you use this approach, make sure you encourage group members to do some of the self-examination exercises suggested throughout the book on their own time.

WHAT'S IN EACH LESSON?

There is one lesson for each of the ten chapters in *Not Even a Hint*. Each lesson contains the following elements to help you dig deeper into the message and apply its truth:

EASY REVIEW

At the beginning of each lesson we've listed the *central issues,* or main points, of the corresponding chapter in *Not Even a Hint* (NEAH). This summary is a great way to quickly refresh your memory about the essence of the chapter. We've also listed a few *key growth objectives* for you so you'll understand what we hope you will *know*, *feel*, and *do* after working through the lesson.

QUESTIONS

The first couple of questions in each lesson are meant to be *discussion starters,* to provide a nonthreatening way to get people talking. Have fun with them.

Most of the remaining questions are either *conceptual* questions, inviting you to deal with ideas or concepts in the book; or *application* questions, guiding you toward putting the concepts into practice in your life. (Many of the questions are preceded by a quote from *Not Even a Hint* to remind you of important principles and to help direct the focus of your discussion.)

Accountability Follow-Up

Near the end of each lesson are two *accountability follow-up* questions, usually relating to the main issues of the preceding lesson. Don't end the meeting until you've checked in on each other's progress in a truthful and caring manner.

Meditate and Memorize

We also list a key Scripture passage, which we encourage you to write out on a card and carry with you during the week. Only when you hide God's Word in your heart will His truth be readily available so that His Spirit can help you gain victory over lust. Ideas for meditating on and memorizing these passages are provided in *NEAH* (158) and in lesson 9 of this study guide.

Custom-Tailored Action Plan

If this study is to help you experience true freedom and victory over sexual temptation, you have to come away with a specific plan of action, and that plan must be tailored uniquely to you. There is no "one size fits all" solution for lust. Every woman's collection of battlefields, strengths, and weaknesses is unique to her.

Beginning with chapter 4 and continuing through chapter 10, you will be guided, step by step, through the formulation of a Custom-Tailored Action Plan, using a simple worksheet on pages 76–9 of the study guide. Your plan is completely flexible—you can revise it whenever and however you wish. And it is designed so that you can easily photocopy it for accountability partners.

HOW TO LEAD A GROUP DISCUSSION ON LUST

Regardless of the size of the group, it's helpful to have one member serve as the leader. She's the one who is responsible to assign the appropriate chapter for the group to read before each meeting, to ask the questions, and to facilitate discussion. If no one else steps up to that role, we encourage you to simply start leading. You don't need a label…just do the job, and the group will function more smoothly and effectively.

Of course, the topic you're tackling is unique. In order to help each other feel safe about sharing honestly, we urge you to take these guidelines seriously:

1. PROMISE AND MAINTAIN CONFIDENTIALITY

In the very first meeting, agree that nothing shared in the group will leave the group without the sharer's permission. (The rare and only exception is information you might need to divulge in order to protect a group member or someone else from harm. If you think this might be the case, seek a pastor's guidance.)

2. CREATE AN ATMOSPHERE OF TRUTHFUL ACCEPTANCE

Each of us is capable of the darkest of sins, and each of us is fighting a hard battle. Group members should listen to one another with compassion and acceptance. This does not mean sacrificing truth, but rather listening with understanding and "speaking the truth in love" (Ephesians 4:15).

3. BE AN EXAMPLE OF HUMBLE HONESTY

Whether you are the designated group leader or not, you can serve the group by stepping out and sharing honestly about your sin and your victories. As friendships and trust develop, you'll encourage others to overcome their fears about sharing by overcoming yours first.

MORE TIPS FOR LEADING A GROUP

1. STRIVE FOR APPLICATION

James 1:22 says, "Do not merely listen to the word, and so deceive yourselves. Do what it says." Remind the women in your group that merely reading a book—even the Bible—and talking about it won't produce change. Real change occurs after we close the book and do something about it. As you progress through the study guide, take time during your meetings to have girls share what changes they've made.

2. START SMALL

While application is important, no one can change in every area all at once. Encourage members of your group to begin by trying to apply just one point from each chapter.

3. OUTLAW ONE-WORD ANSWERS

The questions in the NEAH Study Guide for Women are intended to provoke discussion and even debate. Ban yes and no answers. Encourage women in your group to share openly, not just parrot the "right" answer from *Not Even a Hint*. Giving only expected or "acceptable" answers will not help them examine their own lives.

4. LISTEN TO THE HOLY SPIRIT

This study guide exists to serve you—don't become a slave to it. If one question opens up a fruitful discussion, then go with it! Don't feel you have to work through all of the questions. Take opportunities for the group to pray spontaneously for someone who expresses a need. Let God's Spirit, not this book's format, guide you.

5. ENCOURAGE, ENCOURAGE, ENCOURAGE!

Point out to your friends when you see them growing in a certain area—no matter how small it is. The best way to motivate each other is to acknowledge where God is at work. Offer lots of encouragement.

6. FOCUS ON GOD

In the midst of focusing on the challenge of lust, make sure that the group's primary motive is to please and honor God. Keep reminding each other of the gospel—Christ's death and resurrection has cleansed us from our sins. We've been set free from the rule of sin! Begin and end your time with prayer. Enjoy the journey! Remember, only God's Spirit can work real change in our lives. May God use your study and interaction to bring about life-changing results.

Not Even a Hint

Why Can't I Seem to Beat Lust?

Okay, so you finished chapter 1 of *Not Even a Hint*. How are you doing? If lust is something you have struggled with as a woman, I pray that you would not feel embarrassed. This is an area that all of us face. The only way to fight it is to do exactly what you are doing through this study: humbling yourself to receive God's grace. And remember that God is eager to help you. He is committed to being glorified in your life. You're His daughter! He wants your life to be a reflection of Him. He has paid a great cost—the blood of His Son, Jesus Christ—to forgive you and to free you from your sin.

Begin your study by thanking God for His amazing love for you and for giving you the desire to change.

CENTRAL ISSUES

- Lust defined: craving sexually what God has forbidden.
- There are right and wrong *standards* for holiness, *power sources* for change, and *motives* for fighting sin.
- We're not just against lust; we're *for* God's good plan for sex in marriage.

KEY GROWTH OBJECTIVES

✓ To establish that lust is something we all face in some form.
✓ To understand why God's standard is "not even a hint" of impurity in our lives.
✓ To realize that killing lust leads to the joy and freedom of holiness.

1. In *NEAH*, Josh says that lust is a problem for both women and men. Do you believe this? Why?

2. How does Chelsea's letter (*NEAH* 19–20) make you feel? Why do you think you respond this way?

THE DIFFERENCE BETWEEN LUST AND SEXUALITY

Josh writes, "I have a simple definition for lust: craving sexually what God has forbidden" (*NEAH* 18).

3. What is helpful to you in Josh's definition? What would you change in the definition, if anything? Why?

4. Part of the challenge Christians face in a lust-filled world is remembering that neither sex nor sexuality is our enemy. Lust is our enemy and has hijacked sexuality. We need to keep reminding ourselves that our goal is to rescue our sexuality *from* lust so we can experience it the way God intended (*NEAH* 26).

Summarize from the following Scripture passages the differences between lust and sexuality (see also *NEAH* 25–28).
Lust—Ephesians 5:3; Colossians 3:5; 1 Thessalonians 4:3–4

Sexuality—Genesis 2:22–25; 1 Corinthians 7:2–5

5. It feels as though destroying our lust will destroy us. But it doesn't. And when we destroy our lustful desire, we come not to the end of desire, but to the beginning of *pure desire*—God-centered desire, which was created to carry us into the everlasting morning of God's purposes (*NEAH* 27).

How is God's plan for true satisfaction better than the methods you are sometimes tempted to use?

6. What is an example of you (or someone you know) passing up the instant pleasure offered by lust for a deeper, more lasting joy later? What sacrifice do you think God is calling you *through* for the sake of true joy and godly pleasure?

WINNING GOD'S WAY

There are many different counterfeits that the world offers in the place of God's plan for dealing with lust, but His way is made very clear in the Bible (see *NEAH* 22–25).

God's standard of *not even a hint* quickly brings me to the end of my own ability and effort. It reminds me that God's standard is so much higher than the standards I place for myself that only the victory of Christ's death and resurrection can provide the right power and the right motive needed to change me (*NEAH* 25).

7. Why is God's *standard* of holiness (not even a hint) better than the "diet mentality"?

SHANNON & JOSHUA HARRIS

8. Why is God's *power source* for holiness (the cross of Christ) better than your willpower?

9. Why is God's grace a better *motivation* for holiness than the desire to be seen as good?

10. You're meeting with your friend Katie for lunch. She confides in you, saying, "I love God, but I can't stop going too far physically with the guys I date. I'm afraid they won't like me if I hold back. I keep telling myself that I'll just stop with kissing, but it never ends there. I can't forgive myself, and I'm afraid of what other people think of me."

How will you both encourage and challenge Katie? What clues has she provided about her standard for holiness and her power source and motivation for resisting sin?

FORGIVENESS VERSUS CONDEMNATION

In the preface, Josh writes, "I've learned that I can only fight lust in the confidence of my total forgiveness before God because of Jesus' death for me." If you have put your faith in Christ as your Savior, are you confident of your total forgiveness before God? Do you believe He loves and accepts you because of Jesus' sacrifice for you? Without this confidence it will be difficult to be honest about lust in your life with other carefully selected Christian girlfriends.

11. Share how these passages apply to you:
    1 Timothy 1:15–16

1 John 1:9

Psalm 103:8–13

1 Corinthians 10:13

12. Honesty with others takes courage. Take a minute to talk with God about any fear you have about discussing the topic of lust. Ask His Holy Spirit for courage and a deep hunger for holiness.

ACCOUNTABILITY FOLLOW-UP

Starting with lesson 2, this section will guide your group to review commitments or action points from preceding lessons in order to evaluate your progress and to encourage you toward greater obedience in God's strength. In this first lesson (especially if you're with a group of women you don't know well), use the following questions to begin your journey together.

13. What is one question you would like us to ask you on a regular basis?

14. What is one way you want us to pray for you this week in keeping with this lesson? (Write down each other's requests and take a few minutes to pray for each other.)

MEDITATE AND MEMORIZE

But among you there must not be
even a hint of sexual immorality,
or of any kind of impurity, or of greed,
because these are improper for God's holy people.

EPHESIANS 5:3

What God Called Good

Is It Biology or Is It Sin?

For so many of us women, the world has shaped our understanding of sex. We've learned more from Hollywood than from the Bible. In the world, sexual indulgence is considered normal. If you've sinned sexually, it's easy to wrongly begin thinking of your God-given sexuality as dirty.

Chapter 2 of *NEAH* warns us not to make either mistake. Christian women must embrace the truth that God created sexual intimacy for a husband and wife, and what He created is good. Take a moment and ask God to show you where you have wrong views about sex. Ask Him to reshape them according to His Word.

CENTRAL ISSUES

- God has built into men and women a strong sexual desire, which is pure and good.
- Shame is appropriate when we sin, but misplaced shame distracts us from the real enemy.
- Lust comes out of evil desires in our own hearts and constitutes active rejection of God.
- We must express both gratitude for our sexuality and restraint over lust.

KEY GROWTH OBJECTIVES

✓ To express gratitude for your sexuality.
✓ To soberly acknowledge the danger of lust.
✓ To learn to distinguish between pure sexuality and lust.

1. Describe one or two ways you've gotten the wrong message that sex in itself is bad or that lust is okay.

2. Why do you think these misconceptions are so widely accepted?

THE BEAUTY OF SEXUALITY

In *Not Even a Hint,* Josh writes:

> Our sexuality and our sex drive are intertwined and tied together with our creativity and with our innate human desire to continue life on this spinning planet. Being a sexual being with sexual desires is part of what it means to be a human created in God's image (*NEAH* 34).

3. What does each of the following passages say or assume about your sexuality (see also *NEAH* 33–36)?
   Genesis 1:27–28 and 9:7

   Genesis 2:22–25

   Song of Songs 2:3–4; 4:16; 7:10 (about a married couple)

4. When we break God's commands, shame is appropriate.... [But] misplaced shame can be dangerous because it saps our strength for fighting our real enemy. A person who is wrongly ashamed of being a sexual creature with sexual desires will quickly feel overwhelmed and helpless because he's trying to

overcome more than just lust—he's trying to stop being human! (*NEAH* 36–37).

What do you honestly think of your God-given sexuality most of the time (see also *NEAH* 36–38)?

THE DANGER OF LUST

While rejecting your sexuality is definitely not God's plan, the opposite error of indulging your every desire is sinful (see *NEAH* 38–41).

5. Why is it important to remember the source of lust (James 1:13–14; Matthew 15:18–19)?

6. Why is it important to remember that sexual sin offends God (1 Thessalonians 4:7–8; Psalm 51:4–5)?

7. God says *not even a hint* because you can't give in to lust's demands and hope to pacify it. It always grows. And as it does, lust will rob you of your ability to enjoy true, godly pleasure. You can't bargain with lust and come out a winner (*NEAH* 41).

   What do obedience and true joy look like, according to God? *Ephesians 4:19–24*

   Philippians 1:9–11

8. Though lust longs for an object or a person, ultimately this object is not its prize; its goal is the very *act* of desiring. The result is that lust can never be quenched. As soon as the object of lust is attained, lust wants something more (*NEAH* 41).

REAL LIFE: You drop in on your Christian friend Joan in the neighboring apartment and notice her computer monitor displaying a mildly pornographic web page. She nonchalantly says, "Oh, you know how it is. We all have these sex drives, and I wouldn't be true to myself if I didn't take care of mine now and then."

How will you respond to her? Consider Ephesians 4:19. Where is the "line" she is drawing for herself? How likely will she be to hold that line?

REMEMBERING THE DIFFERENCE

As Christians, embracing our sexuality looks radically different. We don't obey every sexual impulse—nor do we deny that we have sexual desires. Instead, we choose both restraint and gratefulness (*NEAH* 42).

9. Think of a sexual desire or temptation you experienced during the last week or two, and write out what you might have prayed to God in that moment. Express to God both your gratitude for your sexuality and your desire to resist temptation (see Josh's sample prayers on pages 37–38 of *NEAH*).

10. This week, practice responding to sexual desires by quickly turning to God in prayer. (In the next lesson you'll be prompted to look back and reflect on how it went.) Take a moment now and ask the Holy Spirit to help you remember throughout the week the grace and power to obey that He always offers you.

ACCOUNTABILITY FOLLOW-UP

Use these or similar questions to support and encourage each other in your group, or to consider individually before God your progress since your last lesson.

11. How did you do this past week at…
    …*accepting God's standard for holiness (not even a hint)?*

    …*drawing on God's power source for holiness (the cross of Christ)?*

    …*having the right motive in your pursuit of holiness (God's grace)?*

12. How, specifically, can we pray for you or otherwise encourage you?

MEDITATE AND MEMORIZE

> *When tempted, no one should say, "God is tempting me."*
> *For God cannot be tempted by evil, nor does he tempt anyone;*
> *but each one is tempted when, by his own evil desire,*
> *he is dragged away and enticed.*
> JAMES 1:13–14

You Can't Save Yourself

Where Can I Find the Power to Change?

CENTRAL ISSUES

- Legalistic self-sufficiency cannot save us; rather, we are sanctified in God's power *because* He has *already* justified us.
- The gospel is our *power source* for holiness and freedom, and grace is our *motivation*.
- Both legalism and sinful indulgence enslave us; the Holy Spirit can lead us to a life of freedom.

KEY GROWTH OBJECTIVES

✓ To recognize your inability to save yourself.
✓ To understand how justification *empowers* us and grace *motivates* us to be holy.
✓ To learn to rely on the Holy Spirit's power to avoid both legalism and indulgence.

As a woman, I am quite aware that it is in my power to change certain aspects of myself. If I want a new look, I can get a haircut or buy a new tube of lipstick. Any day of the week I can dress funky, classic, or easygoing. If only our sinful desires could be changed as easily as an outfit! Chapter 3 reminds us that becoming holy isn't something we can do on our own.

Are you desperate for change? Remember that you are utterly incapable of changing yourself. Pray that God, who is fully able, will help you and transform you.

1. In *Not Even a Hint,* Josh writes, "Here's what you have to remember: You need to be rescued. You need God's

grace" (*NEAH* 49). How does this compare with what you've been taught by your family, by the media, in school, in church?

2. What honestly comes to mind when you hear the word *holiness*? Why?

YOU'RE NEVER ON YOUR OWN

It's normal for people to want to do things their own way, in their own strength, but…

> …rules and regulations that stem from self-righteous and self-centered motivations can actually take us away from God. John Owen taught that trying to put our sin and lust to death based on our own human strength is the "essence and substance of all false religion in the world." Even a good guideline for fighting lust, if it's "carried out with man-made schemes, always ends in self-righteousness" (*NEAH* 48).

> Legalism is trying to add to what Jesus did when He died and rose again. Legalism is seeking to relate to God based on our work, instead of based on the work of our representative and mediator, Jesus Christ (*NEAH* 49–50).

3. Why is it futile to try in our own strength to achieve salvation (Romans 3:20), or obedience and spiritual growth after salvation (Galatians 3:3)? (See also *NEAH* 47–50.)

4. How does the good news of Jesus' death and resurrection give us *power* for holy living?
   Romans 6:5–8

   Romans 8:1–4

5. How does God's grace provide us with *motivation* to resist temptation?
   Titus 2:11–14

   Hebrews 4:15–16

TRUE FREEDOM, GOD'S WAY

In *Not Even a Hint* (51–52), Josh takes great care to distinguish between our justification and our sanctification.

6. From these Scripture passages, summarize what happens when you are *justified*:
   Romans 3:22–26

   Romans 10:9–10

   Titus 3:3–7

By the way, if you're not certain whether you have received God's forgiveness and been justified in His sight, we encourage you to talk to a pastor or other Christian leader, so that you can be sure.

7. Now read these passages, and describe the process of *sanctification* (the word means "being made holy") in the life of a Christian:
   1 Thessalonians 4:3–5

   1 Thessalonians 5:23–24

8. All the necessary and important aspects of pursuing holiness don't add to our salvation; they're the *response to* and the *result of* God's finished work of justifying us. Christ died so that we could be freed from the hopeless task of trying to justify ourselves (*NEAH* 52).

   Don't doubt your forgiveness. When you feel condemned and separated from God, you're more likely to turn back to lust for comfort, and that's certainly not what God wants you to do. Don't let anything distract you from the rock-solid reality that when God forgives, you're truly forgiven (*NEAH* 53–54).

   If these statements are true, then what *are* the right motives for a Christian's pursuit of sanctification (spiritual growth and victory over sin)?

9. The gospel frees us to do what we were originally created to do: enjoy and glorify God with our whole lives. The gospel sets us free to be holy (*NEAH* 55).

Think of your own life and heart. Describe how holiness manifests itself as freedom for you (see Galatians 5:13–14; Romans 6:16–19; also *NEAH* 54–55).

THE ONE WHO SHOWS THE WAY

The only way we can hope to live a life of holy freedom is under the guidance of God's Holy Spirit (see *NEAH* 55–58).

10. Describe the kinds of freedom God's Holy Spirit can provide when we follow Him.

Romans 8:5–6
Romans 8:26–27
Galatians 5:16–25
(Optional: See also 1 Corinthians 2:11–16; 2 Corinthians 3:17–18)

11. Picture the Spirit-guided life as a proven but narrow path winding between two deep ravines. The safe path of grace and Christian freedom travels between the treacherous pits of legalism on one side and indulgence in sin on the other. For centuries, misguided people have twisted Scripture to justify leaving the path of freedom for one or the other.
    In a similar way, this book you're holding could be misused. One person could apply its practical examples and advice for putting sin to death in a legalistic manner. Another person could take its emphasis on grace and forgiveness as an excuse to indulge in sin (*NEAH* 57–58).

Choose one Scripture passage or one scriptural principle (stated in your own words) that will help you avoid both legalism and indulgence as you complete this series of lessons. Write it down; then stop and invite the Holy Spirit to help you retain this truth in your heart and mind.

ACCOUNTABILITY FOLLOW-UP

Use these or similar questions to support and encourage each other in your group, or to consider individually before God your progress since your last lesson.

12. How did you do during this last week going to God in prayer about your sexual desires? How did you affirm to Him the goodness of your sexuality, as well as the dangers in the temptations you faced?

13. What difference, if any, did these honest prayers make in your ability to resist temptation?

MEDITATE AND MEMORIZE

You, my brothers, were called to be free.
But do not use your freedom to indulge the sinful nature;
rather, serve one another in love.
GALATIANS 5:13

A Custom-Tailored Plan

Where Am I Weakest, and What Can I Do?

CENTRAL ISSUES

- Every woman's vulnerabilities to temptation are unique to her.
- Each of us needs to think through the various times, places, and sources that contribute most strongly to sexual temptation.
- We each need to establish a specific, customized plan, focusing in on one battle at a time.

KEY GROWTH OBJECTIVES

✓ To acknowledge your uniqueness in the battle against sexual temptation.
✓ To help you assess your unique vulnerabilities.
✓ To begin designing a practical plan for dealing with sexual temptation in your life.

Have you ever done the wrong thing and cheated off of someone else's paper? I'm ashamed to admit that I have. It was a state capitals test in high school, and I wasn't prepared. So I got the answers off the girl next to me. I've regretted it ever since.

Why am I confessing this? Because the message of chapter 4 is that we can't "cheat off" someone else's answers to their struggle with lust. We're all different. Two girls—even two sisters—can struggle in totally different ways. That is why we each need a custom-tailored plan for overcoming lust. Be honest about the ways in which you struggle and draw up a plan for action. No cheating, girls!

1. In *Not Even a Hint,* Josh says, "Lust is kept alive and our weaknesses are fortified by the small provisions we give it" (*NEAH* 65). He

describes radical actions people have taken to avoid small concessions to lust—throwing away books and magazines, choosing video rentals through the store window, paying for an unused gym membership. What's your reaction to this? Does it seem overly zealous? Wise? Something else? Why do you say this?

2. What social repercussions might you encounter—among friends, family, fellow students, or coworkers—if you were to take radical action against lust?

YOUR UNIQUE DESIGN

God designed you with your own special personality and your own unique set of strengths (1 Corinthians 12). In similar fashion, you also have your own vulnerabilities (see *NEAH* 62–64).

> Each of us is unique in how we're tempted to lust…. This is why there can be no "one size fits all" approach to combating lust. That's also the reason it would be a mistake to evaluate how you're doing in this area by comparing yourself to others. It's possible to think you're "above lust" just because you're not struggling with it like someone else you know (*NEAH* 62–63).

3. How willing are you to take an honest look at your weaknesses, without comparing yourself to anyone else?

1	2	3	4	5	6	7	8	9	10
I can't handle it									I'm an open book

Why do you think you chose this response?

4. What might help you increase your openness to self-examination by one or two points? (Do you have any concerns about your study group that could be set at ease? Consider praying Psalm 139:23–24.)

5. You know several girls who all have trouble resisting sexually inappropriate sites on the Internet (or some other temptation that you aren't personally tempted by), but since that's not a problem of yours, you're not worried about lust.

Should you worry? Should you adopt some attitude other than worry? Should you take any action? (Consider 1 Corinthians 10:12, a message to you from the God who wants your best and wants to protect you from harm.)

FINDING YOUR WEAK POINTS

My bigger outbreaks of sin are usually triggered by smaller sins that I wasn't diligent in guarding against. I'm talking about the daily, even hourly decisions of what to watch, read, listen to, and allow my mind to think about and my eyes to rest upon (*NEAH* 64–65).

6. Read Romans 13:14. How far should you take "make no provision for the flesh" if you're truly "put[ting] on the Lord Jesus Christ" (ESV)? (Think about the example of Jesus' life [Hebrews 4:14–15].)

7. A lot of people can admit that lust is a prevalent sin in their life and say they want to change. But...they've never taken the time to think through how the process of temptation unfolds for them. Instead of anticipating and being on their guard, they're surprised by the same attack over and over (*NEAH* 62).

    So let's take stock. But first, pause for a moment and invite the Holy Spirit to gently soften your heart and make you sensitive to His guidance.

a. List a few *times* of the day, week, or year that present difficult sexual temptation for you (see *NEAH* 65–66).

b. List a few *locations* that you need to avoid, or where you need to limit your time (see *NEAH* 66–67).

c. Describe any *sources* of sexual temptation that you find difficult to resist (see *NEAH* 67–74; also be sure to consider music and reading material).

CHOOSING WHERE TO STRENGTHEN YOUR DEFENSES

You've read *Not Even a Hint* chapter 4, you've studied a few Scripture passages, and you've examined your own unique lust triggers. But your life will not change until you take action—specific and dramatic action—on what you know, drawing constantly upon God's strength and wisdom.

8. Write a paraphrase of James 1:21–22, inserting the specifics of your unique battle where appropriate.

START YOUR CUSTOM PLAN

Starting with this lesson, and continuing through lesson 10, we will guide you through the completion of a Custom-Tailored Action Plan for dealing with your unique vulnerabilities to lust (see pages 76–9 of this study guide). It is important to remember that the information you write in your Action Plan is totally flexible and can be updated or adjusted as necessary.

We strongly recommend that you make your Action Plan a matter of daily prayer and that you invite one or more trusted Christian sisters to also pray for the specifics of your plan. (The completed Action Plan can easily be photocopied for sharing.)

9. The truth is that we can't deal with everything at once. That's why my advice is to pick one area to begin working on. Choose a specific item from your list to make your focus. Take it to God in prayer. Repent of your apathy toward sin and determine what obedience would look like.

Then seek to be faithful in that area. Take it seriously. Pray about it. Fight the little battles. Flee temptation. As God gives you grace to change in that area, you can move on to another area (*NEAH* 77–78).

Go back over your responses to question 7, praying for wisdom to choose the most strategic lust triggers to address first. Mark one *time* under question a, one *location* under question b, and no more than three *sources* under question c. Transfer these selected items to steps 6 through 8 of your Action Plan (page 77 of this study guide).

10. Ask the Holy Spirit for wisdom, and complete step 9 of your Action Plan, choosing only one lust trigger for focused battle over the next few weeks.

ACCOUNTABILITY FOLLOW-UP

11. Did you recognize God's help this last week as you sought to travel the middle road, avoiding both legalism and sinful indulgence? What happened?

12. What is one way we can support you and pray for you to help you avoid these opposite errors?

MEDITATE AND MEMORIZE

> *But put on the Lord Jesus Christ,*
> *and make no provision for the flesh,*
> *to gratify its desires.*
> ROMANS 13:14, ESV

Guys and Girls

How Are We Different, and How Can We Help Each Other?

CENTRAL ISSUES

- Both men and women battle lust, and all lust is harmful.
- Men and women are "wired" differently sexually, in ways that beautifully complement each other.
- Girls must understand the ways men are sexually tempted and help their male friends not to stumble sexually.
- Unmarried couples must take special precautions in order to preserve their sexual purity for marriage.

KEY GROWTH OBJECTIVES

✓ To correct false gender stereotypes and understand the real differences between men and women.
✓ To understand common sexual pitfalls of men and women.
✓ To learn to dress, speak, and behave around male friends and acquaintances in such a way as to minimize their sexual temptation.

Chapter 5 helps debunk popular misconceptions about male and female sexuality. Do you understand men any better after reading it? More importantly, do you better understand your own struggles with lust? Whether you deal more with longing for emotional intimacy or have strong physical temptations, let's consider how we can treat men as brothers and go the extra mile to make sure we're not generating temptation in the way we act or dress.

1. What if you were listening to the taped session Josh describes in *NEAH* (79–80), and you heard Josh say, "This message is *not* for you!"? Would you listen to the tape anyway? Why?

2. Jack, a twenty-year-old single, writes:

"I think some ladies just aren't aware that even little things can distract guys a lot. When ladies whom I'm friends with dress immodestly, it definitely has a negative effect on our friendship. When a woman dresses immodestly, it makes it difficult to see her as a sister in Christ. There is a constant battle going on as I'm talking with her. Communication becomes more difficult as I'm trying to listen to her, because I'm also trying to fight temptation.

"I heard a story of a Christian girl in my church who went shopping and really liked a shirt she was trying on. But then she thought, *No, I can't do this to the guys.* That was the first time I had ever heard of anything like that, and it made me so grateful. It is such a blessing to have friends who care for us enough to be selfless and to sacrifice what might look attractive in order to help me and other guys with sexual lust. When ladies dress modestly, it's beautiful and makes me want to hang out with them more. I think modesty is so attractive and helpful in friendship because it makes it easier for a friendship to be centered around God and for fellowship to be unhindered."

What do you think of Jack? Would you want to be friends with him? Why? How do you think he would evaluate the clothes you wear?

THE TRUTH ABOUT MEN AND WOMEN

The world is full of deception and misconceptions about the sexual makeup of women and men. Satan loves this, because misinformation keeps us from knowing how to fight the real battles.

3. Isn't it wonderful how God has made men and women to interact with each other? He made men visually oriented, then made women beautiful. He made men initiators, and then designed women to enjoy being pursued.... All this is part of God's wonderful design (*NEAH* 85).

In your own words, describe what is good about God's design for female and male sexuality (see *NEAH 84–85*).

4. In the section "Are All Men Monsters?" (*NEAH 82–84*), Josh writes:

> The truth is that men's lust is more obvious, but not necessarily more sinful. Guys are typically more visually oriented, and as a result their lust is more visible. And because God made men to initiate and pursue women, their expressions of lust are often more aggressive and blatant.... Is a guy's lust, which is blatant and obvious, worse than a girl's lust, which is more refined and subtle? (*NEAH 82–83*).

How would you answer his question?

5. If you, like Kathryn (*NEAH 81–82*), think that you're "the only Christian female" who struggles with physical lust, how does 1 Corinthians 10:13 encourage you? (Or, if you don't struggle with physical lust, how can you show greater empathy for girls who do?)

6. Women, it doesn't matter if your sex drive is as strong as a guy's or how it compares to other girls you know. What matters is whether or not you're looking to God for strength to control the desires you have. What matters is whether or not you're fleeing temptation and pursuing holiness because you love Him (*NEAH 82*).

What is one step you will take in order to invite the help of God and your female friends to control your desires?

HOW GUYS ARE TEMPTED

> Lust blurs and bends true masculinity and femininity in harmful ways. It makes a man's good desire to pursue all about "capturing" and "using," and a woman's good desire to be beautiful all about "seduction" and "manipulation." In general it seems that men and women are tempted by lust in two unique ways: men are tempted by the *pleasure* lust offers, while women are tempted by the *power* lust promises (*NEAH* 85–86).

7. If you identify at all with Josh's description, describe one way that giving in to your temptation might make a guy's battle with temptation even harder (see also *NEAH* 85–88).

8. If you're a woman, you don't have to pose for a picture or star in a pornographic movie to commit pornography. When you dress and behave in a way that is designed primarily to arouse sexual desire in men, you're committing pornography with your life (*NEAH* 87).

Why do Christian women need to carefully consider their dress and behavior?

9. REAL LIFE: You've noticed that at your church group activities, your friend Sonya's way of dressing seems to attract more stares from the guys than usual. On the way to your cars one evening, you mention it to her. She says, "Well, that's their problem. I'm not trying to seduce them. I just wear what makes me feel good about myself."

How will you respond? (What seems to be Sonya's attitude toward her brothers? What desires might she be trying to satisfy by her choices?)

HELPING YOUR GUY FRIENDS

Our membership in God's family must transform our view of the opposite sex. We're not trying to get something from each other: we're called to give, to love, and to care for one another. The opposite sex shouldn't be viewed as a bunch of potential partners—they are men and women created in God's image, whom Christ died to save. They're family! (*NEAH* 94).

10. With what motives and attitudes does God want you to relate to your male friends?
    1 John 3:16

    Romans 14:13

    2 Timothy 2:22

11. Let's get specific about our clothing. We've included a helpful "Modesty Heart-Check" created by Carolyn Mahaney and her daughters (on pages 82–84) that can help us evaluate whether or not we're dressing modestly. After reading the list, do you see any specific areas you feel you should change in the way you dress?

12. Read back over *NEAH* pages 90–92. Brainstorm a few ways you might help your male friends through the ways you interact physically with them (hugs, other touching, body language).

13. From your ideas, choose one or two and transfer them to step 18 of your Custom-Tailored Action Plan on page 79 of this study guide. Take a minute and ask the Holy Spirit to help you put your commitment into practice.

ACCOUNTABILITY FOLLOW-UP

14. How did you do this week dealing with your chosen "lust trigger"? (See step 9 of your Action Plan, page 78 of this study guide.) How did the Holy Spirit help? Other people (accountability partners)?

15. How can we continue to encourage and support you?

MEDITATE AND MEMORIZE

No temptation has overtaken you
that is not common to man.
God is faithful, and he will not let you
be tempted beyond your ability,
but with the temptation he will also
provide the way of escape,
that you may be able to endure it.
1 CORINTHIANS 10:13, ESV

Self-Centered Sex

How Do I Deal with Masturbation?

Josh has received many letters from women admitting that chapter 6 was the first thing they turned to when they picked up *Not Even a Hint*. Women struggle with all the same issues as men, and that includes masturbation. It's an embarrassing topic, for sure, but let's remember that God already knows everything we think and do, and it's His opinion that matters. Let's seek out a woman we can trust and share our sin honestly and completely so we can receive God's grace to change. God will begin to do a work in your heart even as you begin to confess your struggle. Remember the goal: to honor God with every part of our lives and to receive fully the joy that He promises us.

CENTRAL ISSUES

- The battle over masturbation is not the central issue in our spirituality—God is. Masturbation should not be allowed to distract our hearts from centering on Him.
- Still, masturbation is a harmful practice for most or all women, for several reasons.
- There are several practical steps you can take to keep from masturbating and to find restoration after failing.

KEY GROWTH OBJECTIVES

✓ To begin focusing on your relationship with God, rather than on sexual temptation or sin.
✓ To help you think through your own convictions regarding masturbation and God's purpose for sex.
✓ To establish a specific plan to keep from masturbating and to find forgiveness and the power of God's grace after lapses.

1. Does anyone want to be really honest and admit that they turned to this chapter first? Even if you didn't, why do you think so many women have felt compelled to read this chapter first?

2. As you were growing up, what were the standards of your parents or other authority figures regarding masturbation? What emotions were attached to it?

SETTING YOUR HEART ON GOD

As in any area of our lives, God must be at the center of our sexuality (see *NEAH* 99–101).

> I think Christians make too big a deal of masturbation in that we obsess over the act and neglect the more important issues of the heart.... God wants us to be more concerned with the soil of our hearts, out of which a lifestyle of masturbation grows. It's a mistake to make the act of masturbation the measure of our relationship with God (*NEAH* 99).

3. What does God want from you more than anything else (Deuteronomy 6:5; Matthew 22:37–40)? What might this look like as you grow in holiness over the next ten years?

4. God's solution for our guilt is not to change His definition of sin. God dealt with our guilt at the cross of Christ (*NEAH* 100).

How does God deal with sexual sin in your life?

1 Peter 3:18

Romans 6:3–7

5. Lust is a serious sin. Masturbation is one expression of a lustful heart. But when we inflate the importance of this act, we'll either overlook the many evidences of God's work in us or we'll ignore other more serious expressions of lust that God wants us to address (*NEAH* 100–101).

For just a moment, set aside the issue of masturbation. List at least…
    …one area in which God is having victory in your life.

    …one other important area of growth that needs your attention.

Throughout the rest of this lesson, try to keep your focus on loving and pleasing God, rather than on fear and shame. Take a moment now and ask the Holy Spirit to keep you close to Him.

IS MASTURBATION RIGHT OR WRONG?

6. Look back over *NEAH* pages 101–103 and 106, and write a response to each of the following arguments. Use Scripture passages to support your responses whenever possible.

- Argument #1: *Masturbation is a natural, physiological act—it doesn't affect the spiritual* (consider Galatians 5:22–24).

- Argument #2: *I can masturbate without lusting* (consider Jeremiah 17:9).

- Argument #3: *I need masturbation while I'm single; when I'm married, it won't be a problem* (consider 2 Peter 2:19b).

7. First...sex belongs to God. He created our sexuality and is the only One with the authority to dictate how it should be expressed. Sex is for Him. All that we do as sexual creatures should be an expression of our honor, love, and fear of Him.

   Second, a God-centered view of sex strives to honor God's purpose for sex. It's not enough to know God's *rules* for sex. We need to understand his *purpose* and *plan* for it (*NEAH* 104).

What do each of the following passages say about God's purpose and plan for sex (see also *NEAH* 103–106)?

Proverbs 5:15–23

1 Corinthians 7:3–5

Hebrews 13:4

8. How does God's view of sex affect your conviction about masturbation (see *NEAH* 106–108)?

PLANNING AHEAD

9. REAL LIFE: You wake up Saturday morning with no pressing responsibilities awaiting you. As you lie in bed, you recall a sensual dream you had. You pursue your fantasy and you are tempted to masturbate.

   What safeguards do you wish you had in place? Who, among your Christian female friends, could provide support for you?

10. God is after your heart. That's what He cares about. He wants your undivided passion. As your mind is renewed by His Word and as you put away wrong thinking, lust's power will steadily weaken in your life. Set realistic expectations. Complete change will take time and effort (*NEAH* 110).

    With a view toward giving God your fully devoted heart, list several practical ways you might prevent yourself from masturbating (see *NEAH* 108–112).

11. If you fail to resist temptation, what is the best way to love and please God from that moment on?
    Hebrews 4:14–16

1 John 1:9

12. From your ideas in question 9, choose only one or two and transfer them to step 10 in your Custom-Tailored Action Plan on page 78 of this study guide. Take a moment and ask God to give you awareness of His grace, which empowers you to obey.

ACCOUNTABILITY FOLLOW-UP

13. If you are someone who struggles with physical lust, how have you been doing this last week at believing that your impulses are not uncommon? Have you grown in your confidence that God loves and accepts you? That He will help you control your desires?

14. Have you done anything differently lately to make the battle against lust easier for any of your guy friends (see step 18 of your Action Plan)? Tell us about it.

MEDITATE AND MEMORIZE

> *Love the LORD your God with all your heart*
> *and with all your soul and with all your strength.*
> DEUTERONOMY 6:5

Half a Poison Pill Won't Kill You

How Do I Cope with the Temptations of Media?

Girls, I have to admit something: I love a good chick flick! Give me a love story starring a favorite actress, some popcorn, and a bag of Sour Patch Kids, and I'm a happy girl! But I've learned that even seemingly innocent romantic comedies can stir up ungodly longings and desires in a woman's heart and possibly tempt her to be discontent with the season in which God has placed her.

Chapter 7 is a good reminder that if we want to be shaped by God and His Word, we simply *must* be disciplined about our media habits. No person is strong enough to watch TV and movies without being shaped by them. Is your media diet helping or hindering your pursuit of holiness? Take a moment and pray to God, asking Him to help you change your media habits where He sees the need.

CENTRAL ISSUES

- The media can be subtly dangerous because it bypasses reason and goes straight for our affections.
- We must confront our tendencies to justify harmful content and begin to evaluate our entertainment according to godly standards.
- Discernment is more than disapproval—it's *taking action* to change our habits.

KEY GROWTH OBJECTIVES

✓ To become alert to the subtle dangers of the media and to help you assess your attitudes toward the media.
✓ To learn to practice biblical discernment in entertainment choices.
✓ To choose one or two specific steps of action.

1. What do you honestly think of Mrs. Wesley's description of sin in *NEAH* (120)? What is helpful? What would you change?

MEDIA—FRIEND OR FOE?

Nearly all of us grew up with the virtual reality of the entertainment world. That's why the influence of the media can take us by surprise. It helped shape us during our formative years and has been a persistent part of our life experience. Let's do our best to step back and see it for what it really is (see also *NEAH* 115–119).

2. Time for a little quick math—based on an average day, figure out how many hours of TV and/or movies you watch per week, per month, per year. Are you surprised by the amount of time? Do you feel good about it?

3. Television and film stir up feelings and emotions that bypass our minds and go straight for our affections. The incredible power of media is that it can make something evil look good or exciting without appearing to make any argument at all! (*NEAH* 118).

   Describe an instance when a movie or TV show gripped you emotionally—whether it was for good or for harm. What does this say about the sheer power of the media?

4. There's probably not a more important little battle than the daily decisions we make in the area of movies and television (*NEAH* 116).

We need to examine the cumulative effect of our media
habits on our attitude toward God, toward sin, and toward
the world.... They can slowly and subtly undermine biblical
truth and conviction in our hearts (*NEAH* 119).

Choose one popular TV show, and try to identify the
"small" messages it conveys about such topics as authority,
responsibility, integrity, honesty, men and women, sex, God, or
any other important issues. Does this show have a positive or
negative influence on Christian viewers?

EXERCISING DISCERNMENT

It doesn't matter what something is rated, or how popular it
is, or how seemingly innocent it appears. If it hardens your
heart toward God, if it obscures your awareness of the
ugliness of sin and the holiness of God, if it takes the edge
off your spiritual hunger, then it's sin (*NEAH* 120).

5. Summarize how each of these passages can help guide our media
   selections.
   1 Thessalonians 5:21–22

   Ephesians 5:1–4

   Ephesians 5:8–12

   Psalm 101:2–4

6. Choose one movie you've seen recently. With that movie in mind, answer each of the following questions. Briefly explain each answer.

- *Does it increase the strength and authority of your body over your mind (NEAH 120)?*

- *Does it make sin seem attractive to you (NEAH 121)?*

- *Can you honestly thank God for the entire portrayal (NEAH 121)?*

- *Does it promote an evil message or use an evil method (NEAH 123)?*

7. As you work through these questions, you may want to yell "legalism!" But remember, legalism has to do more with the *motive* with which you apply a moral standard than with the standard itself (see lesson 3 and *NEAH* chapter 3). How can these kinds of standards for media selection be compatible with God's grace (consider Galatians 5:13 and Titus 2:11–12)?

TAKING ACTION

We seem to think that because we don't approve [of a movie or show]...we can watch all the garbage in the world and our souls won't be affected. We call this "discernment." But that's as foolish as saying that if you don't enjoy a calorie, it won't make you fat.... If our discernment doesn't lead to appropriate action...it's worthless (*NEAH 122*).

8. REAL LIFE: You and a group of friends—including Stephen, a guy you're attracted to—walk up to a movie theater, undecided about which movie to pick. The consensus suddenly swings toward one that you know will undermine your control over sexual temptation. When you hesitate, Stephen says, "Come on, it's just a movie…not real life."

 You have twenty minutes before showtime. How will you respond to Stephen and the rest? How can you tactfully guard your own heart, and maybe even help your friends guard theirs?

9. "I will set before my eyes no vile thing" (Psalm 101:3). Why? Because I want to know God. I don't want anything to draw my heart away from Him. I want to love holiness.

 Take a moment and talk to God about your love for Him and His love for you. Then brainstorm several steps you might take in order to choose your entertainment more carefully (see *NEAH* 125–127 for ideas).

10. From your ideas in question 9, choose only one or two and transfer them to step 11 in your Custom-Tailored Action Plan on page 78 of this study guide. Ask God for courage and devotion to Him as you face the many small decisions ahead.

 Sometimes we treat entertainment as if it's some kind of right, something essential to our existence. But it isn't. There is no such thing as "must-see TV."… The only thing that's essential is walking with God and pleasing Him. And if that sometimes requires cutting back on what we watch, it's no real sacrifice (*NEAH* 126–127).

ACCOUNTABILITY FOLLOW-UP

11. If applicable, how have your preventative measures for masturbation worked out (see step 10 of your Action Plan)? Do you need to revise your Action Plan? Are you drawing upon God's grace?

12. How close has God been to the center of your heart's affections this last week?

MEDITATE AND MEMORIZE

> *Test everything.*
> *Hold on to the good.*
> *Avoid every kind of evil.*
> 1 THESSALONIANS 5:21-22

Lone Rangers Are Dead Rangers

Why Is Accountability So Important?

Right after I became a Christian, I was planning to leave the local church I'd gotten saved in and move to Nashville. I wanted to be a singer. Why should my new-found faith change my plans? Then God spoke to my heart through the Parable of the Sower in Mark 4. I realized that in order for me to grow, I needed to stay rooted in good soil. The good soil I needed was that of a local church, where I would be surrounded by strong believers, good teaching, fellowship, and accountability. I canceled my plans for Nashville and have never regretted the decision. After reading chapter 8, pray that God would help you develop strong accountability relationships in your local church.

CENTRAL ISSUES

- The Christian life is something we were designed to do together. Find a good local church, take initiative to get involved, and seek accountability relationships.
- Women need accountability as much as men do.
- There are several practical guidelines for accountability.

KEY GROWTH OBJECTIVES

✓ To see the importance of strong Christian fellowship.
✓ To learn a few practical dos and don'ts of accountability.
✓ To establish a specific plan of action.

1. What first comes to your mind when you hear the word
   accountability? How did you develop these impressions?

2. Tell about a past experience you've had with accountability. If it was
   good, tell why. If it was a bad experience, what went wrong?

IS ACCOUNTABILITY FOR ME?

If you cringe at the idea of accountability, it may be because you've
never experienced a positive accountability relationship. Alone, you're
vulnerable. Together we can be strong. (See *NEAH* 133–136, 138–140.)

> Our enemy goes after people who have isolated themselves
> from other Christians. Stragglers make easy victims.
> Without other people to encourage them, watch out for
> them, and confront small compromises in their lives, they
> often end up drifting into serious sin....
>   We need other Christians to speak, sing, and
> sometimes shout the truths of God's Word to us. We need
> others to pray for us when we're in the midst of temptation.
> We need friends who will hold on to us when we're ready to
> give up. We need friends who will challenge and even
> rebuke us when we're indulging in sin (*NEAH* 133–134).

3. According to these passages, why do we need each other?
   Ecclesiastes 4:9–10, 12

   1 Thessalonians 5:14

Hebrews 3:12–13

4. The church is at the center of God's plan; it definitely shouldn't
   be on the outskirts of our lives.... God wants us to be connected
   to a local church and under the spiritual leadership of pastors
   and elders. Without this we won't grow (*NEAH* 135).

Even if you're involved in some other Christian group, why is it
important to become strongly involved in a local church?
Ephesians 4:11–16

Hebrews 10:24–25

5. Please don't think you're the only woman dealing with lust. Don't
   let pride keep you from reaching out for help. You need other
   Christian women to come alongside you. Please don't hide your
   struggle or think that others will look down on you if you confess
   your sin (*NEAH* 139).

Is there anything keeping you from starting an accountability partnership or group? Or keeping you from sharing as honestly as you need
to in your current partnership? How can God and female friends you
trust help with this?

THE BEST WAY TO DO IT

6. Of the five "common mistakes" Josh describes in *NEAH* pages 140–145, which one do you think you will have the hardest time overcoming? Why do you think this is?

7. How can you and your accountability partner(s) go about overcoming this particular mistake together? (Do you need to ask God for humility or courage?)

8. **Repentance involves a change of heart and a decision to turn away from a sin. It's proven over time and involves an ongoing choice to put sin to death (*NEAH* 142).**

   Give an example of one way you might show genuine repentance, not stopping short with confession only.

9. **Often, when a person is confessing sin, they're more aware of their sinfulness than they are of God's grace and mercy. It's a mistake to think that emphasizing guilt will lead to change. The opposite is true. It's only when we remember that God has forgiven our sin because of Jesus Christ that we can find the resolve to keep battling sin (*NEAH* 145).**

   In what area are you likely to experience "gospel amnesia," forgetting God's grace and mercy toward you?
   Stop and talk to God about this, thanking Him for forgiving you. Consider meditating on Psalm 103:8–14.

SETTING UP YOUR ACCOUNTABILITY

10. **Are you willing to clothe yourself with humility and share your struggles with another woman? When you humble yourself and take the step of confessing lust, God will give you more grace to battle that very sin** (*NEAH* 139–140).

    If you don't already have an accountability partner or group, pray for God's guidance. Then think of at least one girl or older woman you would trust. Read back through Josh's suggestions for selecting partners in *NEAH* (136–138). Write here the names that come to mind.

11. Start contacting your potential partners right away to explain your idea and to invite them to begin meeting with you. When you get the number of partners you want (we recommend groups of four or fewer), meet as soon as possible and work out the other details of your accountability relationship. Fill in the details of steps 1–5 in your Custom-Tailored Action Plan (page 76 of this study guide) as you make these decisions.

12. If you already have an accountability partnership or group, complete steps 1–5 in your Custom-Tailored Action Plan. Choose one or two of Josh's suggestions to discuss with your partner or group, looking for ways to keep your interaction as beneficial as possible.

ACCOUNTABILITY FOLLOW-UP

13. How have your plans for carefully selecting your entertainment helped you this week (see step 11 of your Action Plan)?

14. How can we encourage and support you?

MEDITATE AND MEMORIZE

> *And let us consider how we may spur one
> another on toward love and good deeds.*
> HEBREWS 10:24

The Sword of the Spirit

How Can the Truth Help Me Defeat the Lies?

Every day you're flooded with the powerfully alluring lies of the world. They tell you how to view yourself as a woman. They tell you that sin is no big deal. Sometimes they may seem overwhelming. But as chapter 9 helped us see, the promises of God's Word are even greater. And God doesn't lie.

Before you start this lesson, ask God to fill you with conviction that His Word is true, living, and powerful and to give you a hunger for Himself and His Word.

1. Tell about a true statement you learned as a child (from the Bible, your parents, a teacher) that has proven helpful in a time of need.

CENTRAL ISSUES

- Reading, meditating on, and memorizing God's Word fills us with life-giving truth that protects us from worldly lies about sex.
- For every lie about sex, there is scriptural truth that addresses it.
- Dwelling on God's truth helps us remember that the pleasures of God are far greater than the pleasures of lust.

KEY GROWTH OBJECTIVES

✓ To understand the importance of God's living Word in your daily life.
✓ To apply at least one scriptural truth to a lie you struggle with now.
✓ To establish a specific plan for memorizing and applying God's Word in your daily life.

2. What is one reason you might forget you're involved in a life-and-death spiritual battle?

THE POWER OF A PROMISE

Let's look at the importance of God's Word in our daily lives (see *NEAH* 147–151).

My goal is to do more than just suggest a few memory verses—I want to help you develop a *conviction* that Scripture is the only weapon that can successfully fight off lust.

Can you imagine how foolish it would be for a soldier to go into battle without his weapon or for him to let it fall into disrepair? As Christians, it's just as foolish for us to fight lust without the only offensive weapon God has given us (*NEAH* 150).

3. According to these passages, why is God's Word essential to your daily life?
   Ephesians 6:10–13, 17

   Hebrews 4:12

   Psalm 119:32

4. Scripture cuts through the confusion and hazy half-truths that our sin generates. It reveals our wrong desires. It rebukes our apathy. It corrects our selfish human thinking. It unmasks the deception of sin. It points us to God's goodness and faithfulness when we're tempted to forget. It trains us in righteousness. It counters the false promises of lust with God's true promises (*NEAH* 151).

What does God Himself say His Word does for us?
Psalm 119:9–11

Psalm 119:92–93

Psalm 119:104–105

2 Timothy 3:16–17

1 John 2:14

5. Stop for a moment and think about your attitude toward the Bible.
   How strongly do you depend on God's Word in your daily life?
   How much do you hunger for the heart of God, which is revealed
   in His Word?

CLAIMING THE PROMISE

Now let's practice applying God's Word to a lie with which you've struggled
recently.

6. Look over the lies Josh has listed in *NEAH* (pages 152–157), and
   think about any other lies that you've been tempted by lately.
   Choose one that you'd like to address, and write it here, using any
   wording you wish.

LIE of Lust:

7. Stop and ask God for wisdom to deal with this lie. Find a passage of Scripture that reveals the lie for what it is and supplies the truth instead. You might find it among those Josh has suggested (*NEAH* 152–157), or you might find it by using a concordance or a Bible dictionary, or by asking a pastor or other Christian leader. When you find it, write it out below.

TRUTH of God's Word:

8. Now take a few minutes to meditate and pray over the passage. Several ways to do this are listed. Use whichever ideas are most helpful to you.

• Read the passage aloud several times, emphasizing different words or phrases each time. Think about why God chose to word the passage this way.
• Think about the differences between this truth and the lie you've written above.
• If appropriate, insert your name and personalize the passage.
• Think about the implications of the passage in your life, especially as it addresses the lie you've written above.
• Ask God for the power to apply this truth and to resist the lie. Request His help with specific actions and decisions.
• Praise and thank God for the changes He will make in your heart as He engraves this truth on it.

By practicing biblical meditation on a Scripture passage, focusing on its meaning and application, you'll discover that memorization comes much more easily. Now you're memorizing meaning, not just words. You're relating directly to God, not just to a page in a book.

The key to holiness is satisfaction in God—faith that He is more to be desired than anything this world has to offer. We're not just turning away from lust; we're turning toward true satisfaction and joy in God....

The Inventor of all good pleasure has eternal pleasures waiting for you and me that we can't imagine or anticipate. All the experiences of pleasure we've known in this life are but faint echoes of what He has for us there (*NEAH* 158–159).

GOD'S WORD IN MY HEART

9. REAL LIFE: You're at coffee again with Katie (your friend from lesson 1). She is doing much better at drawing the line at *not even a hint* in her physical relationships with guys, and she's doing it now with the power source and motive in mind. "I love God," she says, "and I'm relying on His power and grace, but His power doesn't seem to be coming through for me. I can't always resist the way He says He will help me to." You ask how much Bible reading and memorization she's doing, and she confesses that it has been almost nil.

   What specific guidance will you give her? Which passages would you suggest, and how can she integrate them into her heart and mind?

10. Now for your own plan. Go through Josh's list of Scripture passages in *NEAH*, pages 152–157, along with any other passages you might consider hiding in your heart. Choose the first five you want to memorize, and write them under step 14 of your Custom-Tailored Action Plan on page 79 of this study guide. Mark the passage you'll start with.

11. Now think about the best times, places, and methods for your memorization plan. Consider Josh's suggestions in *NEAH* (page 158), as well as the meditation exercise in question 8. Then fill in steps 15–17 of your Action Plan.

ACCOUNTABILITY FOLLOW-UP

12. Have you made progress toward establishing an accountability partnership? Or, if you're already in one, are you making the most of the partnership for your growth and holiness?

13. What about the *other* parts of your Action Plan to date? Is there an area in which you've experienced victory, or one for which you'd like our focused prayer?

MEDITATE AND MEMORIZE

How can a young [woman] keep [her] way pure?
By living according to your word.
I have hidden your word in my heart
that I might not sin against you.
PSALM 119:9, 11

Holiness Is a Harvest

How Can I Sow to the Spirit?

I turned thirty this year. On this birthday, I thought a lot about the godly, humble, and Scripture-infused woman I want to be and whether or not I was on the right track for that goal.

As I assessed myself, I realized that some of the small day-to-day choices I make do not add up to my becoming that woman. The endless barrage of catalogs, magazines, and the distraction of the Internet lead to lost opportunities. The time wasted on these pursuits could have been spent filling myself with Living Water, or building relationships, or serving a need. If I want to reach that goal at the end of my life, I have to choose day by day, hour by hour, and moment by moment to sow to the Spirit.

After you read chapter 10, take a moment to ask God to give you faith for a lifelong pursuit of holiness. Ask Him to fill you with excitement at His promise of a coming harvest of righteousness.

CENTRAL ISSUES

- The principle of the harvest (Galatians 6:7–9) requires diligence and daily dependence on God's grace.
- Rather than making resistance to sexual temptation our primary preoccupation, we should focus on sowing to the Spirit in order to ensure a harvest of holiness.

KEY GROWTH OBJECTIVES

- ✓ To recognize the reality of the harvest principle in your life.
- ✓ To make sowing to the Spirit your priority.
- ✓ To establish a specific plan for sowing to the Spirit.

1. See if you can devise a commercial jingle or slogan to sell sin by convincing your audience that they will reap no consequences. Can you identify the error in this marketing logic?

2. Do you have any important questions related to lust that this study guide has not helped you answer? How might you find help with these questions? (Consider talking to a pastor, a Christian counselor, or some other Christian leader.)

RECOGNIZING THE HARVEST PRINCIPLE

There are two fields before each of us and two kinds of seeds we can plant (see *NEAH* 161–165).

> **What you see in your spiritual life today is the direct result of what you've put in the soil of your life in days past. We can't get around this truth. There are no exceptions—our actions and choices can't be separated from specific consequences** (*NEAH* 163).

3. Read Galatians 6:7–9. List below three small sinful indulgences you are likely to be tempted by in the next few days. Then describe the harvest that comes from such sowing.

Small sinful indulgences   *The harvest (consequences)*

_____   _____

_____   _____

_____   _____

4. **We want to stop sowing seeds to the flesh. But that's not all we should do. Even more, we want to sow seeds in the field of righteousness** (*NEAH* 164).

    Now list three small ways you can sow to the Spirit in the next few days, along with the harvest it will produce.

Small ways of sowing to the Spirit   *The harvest (spiritual fruit in your life)*

   _____   _____

   _____   _____

   _____   _____

5. Now read carefully through Galatians 5:16–25. Summarize this passage's message in two to four sentences.

6. REAL LIFE: You're on the phone with your friend Jenna. "I keep having these inappropriate thoughts about the guys here at work and in my apartment building," she confides. "Why can't I keep my thoughts pure? I haven't done anything really bad." As you talk further, you learn that Jenna still fills her spare time reading romance novels—during work breaks, downtime at home, at bedtime.

    How will you encourage her toward freedom? How is she sowing to and reaping from the flesh? How could she be sowing to and reaping from the Spirit?

CHOOSING HOW TO SOW

As Josh explains in *NEAH* (pages 165–170), there are hundreds of ways to sow to the Spirit, but a few habits are especially critical.

> I believe that communing daily with God through reading His Word, through prayer, and through self-examination is among the most essential ways we can sow to the Spirit....
>
> The greatest privilege of my life isn't writing or speaking or being a pastor—it is relating to, communicating with, and knowing the Creator of the universe.... There is nothing more wonderful! And there's nothing more important in our fight against lust (*NEAH* 166–167).

7. How does each of these passages describe the highest priority and privilege in our lives?
   Psalm 27:4, 8

   Psalm 73:25–26

   John 17:3

   Philippians 3:7–14

8. What will it take in your life to make your devotional time with God the number one priority of your day? Do you need to cut back or eliminate some competing activity?

I don't think we should make overcoming lust our primary
preoccupation—we need to make the gospel and God's
glory our focus. We need to give ourselves to knowing Him,
worshiping Him, and meeting with Him every day. The result
will be the weakening of lust and a growing passion for
godliness (*NEAH* 169–170).

REAPING THE HARVEST FOR LIFE

You will only succeed at making daily time with God your priority if
you also make a plan and take it seriously.

9. Describe the best time and place for your daily time with God.

10. How could you use that daily time? Which books of the Bible
   might you start reading? What might you pray for? What habits of
   self-examination could you establish?

11. Pray over the ideas you've raised in questions 9 and 10, asking God
   for wisdom. Then complete steps 12 and 13 in your Custom-
   Tailored Action Plan on page 78 of this study guide. (Remember,
   you can revise your plan as needed.)

If you have worked through this entire study guide, you should now have a completed Action Plan. We recommend that you give copies to your accountability partners. Read your plan every day, and use it as a guide for daily prayer. Celebrate every small and large victory, and seek God's forgiveness when you disobey.

Don't give up! God has a beautiful harvest of holiness in store for you (Galatians 6:9). And remember that your power source is the cross of Christ.

> Remember, God doesn't call you to sacrifice as an end in itself. He calls you through it. On the other side of sacrifice is unspeakable beauty and indescribable joy. It's not easy, but it's worth every minute.
> So welcome to the persevering fight. Welcome to the mystery of dying to yourself and finding real life. Welcome to the pleasure and freedom of holiness (*NEAH* 172).

ACCOUNTABILITY FOLLOW-UP

12. Have you started meditating on and memorizing a new Scripture passage this week (or continued work on one)? How is it going? Do you need to revise your Action Plan in any way (see steps 14–17 on page 79)?

13. At this point in your life, how can we most effectively pray for you as you sow to the Spirit?

MEDITATE AND MEMORIZE

Do not be deceived: God cannot be mocked.
A man reaps what he sows.
The one who sows to please his sinful nature,
from that nature will reap destruction;
the one who sows to please the Spirit,
from the Spirit will reap eternal life.
Let us not become weary in doing good,
for at the proper time we will reap a
harvest if we do not give up.
GALATIANS 6:7-9

Custom-Tailored
Action Plan

You will find the guidelines for completing this plan in lessons 4–10 of this study guide.

Keep in mind: This plan is *completely flexible*. It can change as you grow.

This worksheet is designed for easy photocopying for yourself or for accountability partners.

MY PLAN FOR ACCOUNTABILITY (LESSON 8)

1. Name(s) of my accountability partner(s):

2. When and how often we will communicate:

3. How and where we will communicate (meeting, phone, e-mail):

4. What I want to be asked (simply walking through this completed worksheet is one option):

5. How we will ensure follow-up (so that past commitments won't be forgotten):

MY LUST TRIGGERS (LESSON 4)

Consider making this page a daily prayer list for yourself and your accountability partner(s).

6. One time of day I'm especially susceptible to temptation:

7. One type of location that presents strong temptation for me:

8. Sources of strong sexual temptation for me (for example, TV, newspaper, magazines, music, books, Internet, mail—*list no more than three at a time*):

9. From among 6–8 above, the *one* trigger I choose for focused battle now (in God's grace and strength):

DEALING WITH MASTURBATION (LESSON 6)

10. My action step(s) *(no more than two):*

Don't forget God's forgiveness and power for change (see 1 John 1:9).

DEALING WITH THE MEDIA (LESSON 7)

11. My action step(s) *(no more than two):*

SOWING TO THE SPIRIT (LESSON 10)

12. The time and place for my daily devotional time with God:

13. What I will do during that time (where in Scripture I'll read, what I'll pray for, how I'll examine myself):

GOD'S TRUTH TO ANSWER THE WORLD'S LIES (LESSON 9)

14. Five Scripture passages for my meditation and memorization (*add more as needed*):

15. How I will do my meditation and memorization:

16. When and how often:

17. Where:

HELPING MY MALE FRIENDS AVOID SEXUAL TEMPTATION (LESSON 5)

18. My action step(s) (*no more than two*):

Discussions about modesty aren't that helpful if we're not willing to get practical and specific. I think the following list by Carolyn Mahaney and her daughters (all dear friends of mine!) covers the main issues we ladies face with today's clothing. I appreciate their straightforward approach and encourage you to apply these tests to your own wardrobe. If you're looking for more on modesty, I recommend a booklet by Nancy Leigh DeMoss called *The Look: Does God Really Care What I Wear?* To order, call (800) 321-1538, or visit www.LifeAction.org.

A Modesty Heart-Check for Girls

by Carolyn Mahaney, Nicole Whitacre, Kristin Chesemore,
and Janelle Mahaney

Women should adorn themselves in respectable apparel,
with modesty and self-control, not with braided hair
and gold or pearls or costly attire,
but with what is proper for women who
profess godliness—with good works.
1 TIMOTHY 2:9–10, ESV

START WITH A HEART CHECK

- What statement do my clothes make about my heart?
- In choosing what clothes to wear today, whose attention do I desire and whose approval do I crave? Am I seeking to please God or impress others?
- Is what I wear consistent with the biblical values of modesty, self-control, and respectable apparel, or does my dress reveal an inordinate identification and fascination with sinful cultural values?
- Who am I trying to identify with through my dress? Is the Word of God my standard, or is the latest fashion?
- Have I solicited the evaluation of other godly individuals regarding my wardrobe?
- Does my clothing reveal an allegiance to the gospel, or is there any contradiction between my profession of faith and my practice of godliness?

Before you leave the house, a modesty check. *What are some things I should look for as I stand in front of my mirror?*

FROM THE TOP...

- When I am wearing a loose-fitting blouse or scoop neck, can I see anything when I lean over? If so, I need to remember to place my hand against my neckline when I bend down.
- If I am wearing a button-down top, I need to turn sideways and move around to see if there are any gaping holes that expose my chest. If there are, I've got to grab the sewing box and pin between the buttons.
- The same check is needed if I am wearing a sleeveless shirt. When I move around, can I see my bra? If I do, I need the safety pins again!
- Am I wearing a spaghetti-strap, halter, or sheer blouse? Not even pins will fix this problem! Most guys find these very unhelpful in their struggle with lust. It's time to go back to the closet.
- Can I see the lace or seam of my bra through my shirt? In this case, seamless bras are a better option.
- More Key Questions: Does it reveal any part of my cleavage? Does my midriff show when I raise my hands above my head? Is my shirt just plain too tight? If the answer to any one of these questions is yes, then I need to change my outfit.

MOVING ON DOWN...

- Does my midriff (or underwear) show when I bend over or lift my hands? If so, is it because my skirt or my pants are too low? Either my shirt needs to be longer or I need to find a skirt or pants that sit higher.
- I also have to turn around to see if what I'm wearing is too tight around my backside, or if the outline of my underwear shows. If so, I know what I have to do!
- And as for shorts—I can't just check them standing up. I need to see how much they reveal when I sit down. If I see too much leg, I need a longer pair.
- The "sit-down" check applies to my skirt or dress as well. And I must remember to keep my skirt pulled down and my knees together when I'm seated.

- And speaking of skirts, watch out for those slits! Does it reveal too much when I walk? Pins are also helpful here.
- Before I leave, I need to give my skirt a "sunlight check." Is it see-through? If so, I need a slip.
- Finally, I must remember to do this modesty check with my shoes on. High heels make my dress or skirt appear shorter.

And don't forget—this applies to formal wear as well.

A note on swimwear—it's not easy, but you can still strive to be modest at the pool or beach. Look for one-piece bathing suits that aren't cut high on the leg or have a low neckline.

Purity Download

Seven Tips for On-Line Purity

BY JOSHUA HARRIS

The Internet is a wonderful tool. We can use it to work, to study, even to share the gospel with people in other parts of the world. But if we're not careful it can become a door to great sin and spiritual ruin. Many Christian women have fallen prey to the temptation of lust on-line—through pornography or illicit conversations in chat rooms. It's instantly accessible and easily hidden from others. But God sees all our sin. And Internet impurity will always lead to heartache and regret. Whether or not this is a current area of temptation for you, the following seven tips will equip you to honor God on-line.

1. IDENTIFY WHAT'S LEADING UP TO LUSTFUL INDULGENCE ON THE INTERNET.

For many women, sin on-line is preceded by compromise in areas such as their fantasies, television viewing, or reading material. It might seem like sexual sin on-line "comes out of nowhere," but it's often something we build up to through disobedience in other areas. Prayerfully consider where you can be fighting these little battles more diligently.

2. RESOLVE THAT NO TECHNOLOGICAL CONVENIENCE IS WORTH SINNING AGAINST GOD.

Most people have to use the Internet for school or work. But we should never place the convenience of technology above God's commands for holiness. If you've struggled with Internet porn, be willing to take radical action. Maybe that means no Internet access at your home for a season. Or not having high-speed access. It could mean going on-line only when you're with other people or deciding to completely avoid chat rooms. My dad has only one computer in his house with a web browser, and that computer is in the middle of the living room. But that's not all…my mom is the only one with the password to get onto it! Inconvenient? Incredibly so! But he's more concerned with protecting himself and my younger brothers than with convenience.

3. EXAMINE YOUR MIND-SET WHEN BROWSING AND THE AMOUNT OF TIME SPENT ON-LINE.

If Internet use has become a mindless entertainment activity, where your brain goes into neutral, you're in dangerous territory. You might not be struggling with Internet porn right now, but there's a good chance that this mind-set will lead to compromise. Go on-line with a purpose. And don't spend tons of time browsing aimlessly. Cutting back so that the time you spend on-line is focused and has a point will significantly cut back on the temptation to slip into the darker corners of the Web.

4. HAVE AN ACCOUNTABILITY PARTNER THAT CONSISTENTLY ASKS ABOUT YOUR INTERNET ACTIVITY.

Even if you don't have a history of struggling with lust on-line, we should all have a friend who regularly asks how we're doing in this area. Find someone and get her to commit to bringing up the subject consistently.

5. MAKE YOUR DEFINITION OF "OVER THE LINE" FAR FROM THE EDGE OF THE CLIFF.

Susan has been struggling with temptation to look at on-line porn for a week. She's been stretching her resolve by visiting somewhat questionable sites and the urge to indulge is growing. Unfortunately, she doesn't share this with her accountability partner. Instead she battles in secret. But a week later she "really messes up" and spends two hours browsing illicit sites. Do you see the problem? Susan's definition of "over the line" when it comes to sin is right at the edge of the cliff—when she finally confesses she's already fallen.

When it comes to accountability, I think it's important to back up our definition of blowing it on-line. We need to involve others much earlier in the process of temptation. So confess when you're dabbling with somewhat questionable sites (or okay sites with provocative ads). Share when you're spending too much time on-line. Make these things your definition of messing up so your friends can pray for you and challenge you long before you slip off the edge of temptation. Thomas Watson once wrote, "A godly man will not go as far as he may, lest he go further than he should."

6. USE WEBSITE FILTERS, BLOCKERS, AND ACCOUNTABILITY SOFTWARE AS A FINAL LINE OF DEFENSE, NOT THE FIRST.

Programs that e-mail a list of all the websites you visit or block bad content are a wonderful tool. But they can't replace a heart that truly hates sin and desires to please God. Utilize them *after* you've taken a look at your heart and examined the lies you tell yourself in the process of temptation. Do the work of digging into God's Word, meditating on Scripture, making yourself accountable, and other steps listed above. Blocking and accountability software can then serve to support your heart convictions instead of trying to substitute them.

7. FIGHT THIS SIN THE HARDEST WHEN YOU'RE FEELING STRONG.

Many people experience a level of "victory" over Internet porn for a season—only to be lulled into a false sense of security and fall again. If you're experiencing a time of relative freedom from the sin of Internet pornography, that's good…but don't stop watching this part of your life carefully. It's when you're feeling strong that you should fight the hardest. In other words, kick sin when it's down. Redouble your grace-motivated efforts. Keep "backing up" your definition of on-line compromise. Memorize Scripture. Pray for God's power. By doing so you'll weaken the power of this sin in your life even more.

Joshua and Shannon Harris have been happily married for five years. They live outside Washington, D.C., in Gaithersburg, Maryland. Josh is a pastor at Covenant Life Church. Shannon is a homemaker and is mommy to Emma and Joshua Quinn. (Shannon has the more demanding job!) Shannon is also a gifted vocalist who uses her talent on the church worship team as well as on worship recordings from Sovereign Grace Ministries. She wrote the introductions to all the chapters for this study guide.

For more information about Josh's other books and updates on his speaking schedule visit:

www.joshharris.com

You can also write:

Joshua Harris
P.O. Box 249
Gaithersburg, MD 20884-0249

Not Just for Women

JOSHUA HARRIS

WITH BRIAN SMITH

A STUDY GUIDE FOR MEN

not *even* a hint

Overcoming lust is a process that requires diligent focus and accountability from others. This guide helps establish both. This guide is designed for both individual use as well as small group settings—from one-on-one accountability partners to Sunday school classes. This study guide is gender specific so that questions and study questions can be more pointed and addressed specifically to the unique temptations that men face.

ISBN 1-59052-253-2

Tired of the game?
Kiss dating goodbye.

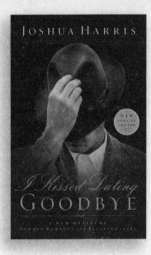

I KISSED DATING GOODBYE

Dating. Isn't there a better way? Reorder your romantic life in the light of God's Word and find more fulfillment than the dating game could ever give—a life of purposeful singleness.

ISBN 1-59052-135-8

I KISSED DATING GOODBYE VIDEO SERIES

Three-video series   ISBN 1-59052-180-3
Video-Part 1: Love   ISBN 1-59052-212-5
Video-Part 2: Purity ISBN 1-59052-213-3
Video-Part 3: Trust   ISBN 1-59052-214-1

I KISSED DATING GOODBYE STUDY GUIDE

The *I Kissed Dating Goodbye Study Guide*, based on Joshua Harris's phenomenal bestseller provides youth with a new resource for living a lifestyle of sincere love, true purity, and purposeful singleness.

ISBN 1-59052-136-6

Say Hello to Courtship

This dynamic sequel picks up where *I Kissed Dating Goodbye* left off. Joshua and Shannon Harris share their inspiring experience of how a joyous alternative to recreational dating—biblical courtship—worked for them. *Boy Meets Girls* helps couples journey from friendship to marriage while avoiding the pitfalls of today's often directionless relationships. It gives practical advice about communication, involving your family in your relationship, keeping your relationship pure, dealing with past sexual sin, and the questions to ask before you get engaged.

ISBN 1-57673-709-8